IRELAND

A PICTURE BOOK TO REMEMBER HER BY

© Illustrations:
Colour Library Books
Designed and Produced by
Ted Smart and
David Gibbon CLI.
Published 1977.
Filmsetting by Focus Photoset Ltd.,
90-94 Clerkenwell Road, London EC1R 5DL.
Printed by I.G. Domingo and bound by Eurobinder,
Barcelona (Spain)
All rights reserved.
ISBN 84-499-5062-7
CRESCENT 1978

Camlough, Co. Armagh *top left.* Below Camlough Mountain lies the narrow expanse of water from which this picturesque beauty spot takes its name.

A cottage *bottom left,* typical of the area, in Co. Fermanagh.

Standing some two miles west of Bushmills, Co. Antrim are the picturesque ruins of Dunluce Castle *above.* The castle was built in the 14th century on a detached rock far above the sea. It was eventually allowed to fall into disuse following the restoration of Charles II.

The Mountains of Mourne, *overleaf* made famous in song as they sweep down to the sea, are the highest mountain range in the six Northern Counties. From the summit of the highest, Slieve Donard, magnificent views of the surrounding countryside are to be seen.

Overlooking the sea, and outlined against the sky, stand the ruins *left* of Dunluce Castle in Co. Antrim, Its air of decay lends it a romantic air. Two of the original five circular towers still remain to tell of its former glory.

South of the centre of Belfast in University Street stands the wonderful old Tudor style building of Queen's University *above* with its square tower. Founded in 1849, it became a separate University in 1908 and now incorporates excellent, up-to-date teaching facilities.

Lough Neagh *top right* is the largest stretch of inland water in Great Britain. Sheltered at the eastern end by the hills of Belfast, it lies in picturesque surroundings and is traditionally said to have been formed by the overflowing of a fountain. Coney Island which lies at the south-west extremity of the Lough has associations with St. Patrick.

The fine beaches near Portrush *above* are intriguing with their beautiful caves and strange rock formations. Looking out to the Atlantic, Portrush, on its basalt peninsula, is a favourite resort with its dramatic views of the Donegal mountains to one side and the many islands on the other. On a clear day the Mull of Kintyre in Scotland can be seen.

Kenbane Castle *bottom right* stands some 3½ miles north-west of Ballycastle. It was built by Colla McDonnell in 1547, attacked by the English and finally captured and sacked in 1551 by Sir Thomas Cusack. Later it was restored and re-occupied by Colla and, on his death in 1558, passed to his younger brother, the renowned Sorley Boye McDonnell of nearby Dunanynie. It is now in the charge of the Antrim County Council.

The pretty harbour of Ballintoy village *below* looks out to Rathlin Island, the stocking-shaped island and stepping stone to Scotland. A grassy path leads off to the west to Whitepark Bay, paradise for naturalists and archaelogical enthusiasts. To the east is Carrickarade Island, linked to the mainland by a fearsome rope bridge.

Carrickfergus is a few miles south of Larne, terminal of the shortest sea route from Britain. The Castle *top right* built by the Normans, has been restored to keep its original 13th century character. Within its ramparts King John, Edward Bruce, Con o'Neil of Clandeboye and many others have played their part in history and legend.

The village of Bushmills *bottom right* is situated on the river Bush which provides excellent fishing. It is not far inland from the pleasant beach of Portballintrae. However the mills, the nine-hole golf course and the fishing all pale in comparison with the quality of the whiskey they make in the Bushmills distillery.

Situated on the low-lying Ards Peninsula, the famous Ballycopeland Windmill *right* is one of the few mills in existence in Ireland. It is believed to date from the 16th century and has wooden parts, still in working order. Nearby Carrowdore Castle was the home of the Huguenot family who introduced the linen industry to Ireland.

The village of Dundrum *top left* stands on the shores of Dundrum Bay. An attractive little fishing port, it has the ruin of an historic castle. The keep is circular and is a magnificent vantage point from which to view the beautiful surrounding scenery and the Mourne Mountains which lie some few miles to the south-west.

Kilkeel *bottom left,* the Church of the Narrow, is an attractive and prosperous resort with a beautiful beach and busy fishing and yachting harbour. At one time it was the capital of the erstwhile Kingdom of Mourne and affords excellent views of the magnificent lofty mountains with their fine scenery and silent loughs.

A famous port in the Middle Ages, Ardglass *below* is now a centre of the herring fishing industry. Colonised by the English at the time of Henry IV, the town was surrounded by a ring of castles many of which, although now in ruins, can still be seen. Jordan's Castle is well preserved and is open to the public.

The curving arm of the rocky outcrop that supports the town forms a shelter for the beach of Portstewart Strand *above*. The town is proud possessor of two eighteen hole golf courses. Although the temperature is not always suitable for swimming, the white beach and blue waters always invite one to pause and admire.

Londonderry derives its name from the granting of the city to a body of London merchants. It was previously known as Derry-Columbkille after St. Columba who founded a monastery on the site in 546. The Guildhall *right* rebuilt in 1908, the previous building having been destroyed by fire, has a fine bell tower and several interesting stained glass windows presented by the London Companies.

The magic of Ireland is ever present as dusk falls on Kesh Bay *below left*. Nearby the stone circles of a Bronze Age temple stand as they have for centuries. Though Kesh boasts of a sailing school and three ski clubs, these do not ruffle the waters of the lake as often as the ducks and fish which abound among the islands.

Barnes Gap *above,* famed for its lovely scenery, is a three-mile cleft through the mountains between the winding Glenelly and Owenkillew river valleys. Though peaceful now, this was the land of highwaymen and kidnappers and in the Sperrin mountains on the far side of the Glenelly, the last wolf in Ireland was shot two centuries ago.

To the south of Lough Erne, in the heart of the Irish lake district, stands Monea Castle *right* which is named Ma Nia—the Plain of Heroes. The castle is a splendid example of the fortified homes built by the Scottish and English settlers and the well-preserved structure features the crow-stepped gables reminiscent of Scotland.

The famous Mourne Mountains *above,* rendered immortal in
song and verse, are the highest in Northern Ireland.
Dominated by Slieve Donard, 2,796 ft., which rises to the
south-west of Newcastle, the tallest peaks command a fine
view, on a clear day, across the Irish Sea to the Isles of
Arran and Man.

The name Portrush is derived rom the Gaelic 'Port Rois' meaning Harbour of the Headland and the town is indeed situated on the rocky Ramore Head *below* jutting almost a mile out into the sea. The peninsula is believed to have been the site of an English fort as it was at one time sold to an English adventurer for 'a hogshead of claret yearly'.

Lying in the outer waters of Galway Bay are the Aran Islands, Galway. Consisting of three islands, Inishmore–The Great Island, Inishmaan–The Middle Island and Inisheer–The Western Island, they face the harsh Atlantic and are thus windswept and largely bare. The islands are a particular source of interest to seekers of pre-Christian and medieval antiquities. Fishing forms the main occupation of the hardy islanders although some crops are grown in small areas.

The upper reach of Dungarvan harbour *above* and Knockmealdown Mountains, Co. Waterford. The mountain range follows the border between Tipperary and Waterford for some distance and affords some fine views. In Dungarvan the remains of the Castle keep, originally the work of King John, may still be seen.

A small seaside resort, Annestown *above right* lies in Dunabrattin Bay. The ruins of the 17th century Dunhill Castle are nearby.

Waterford, Co. Waterford *right* was originally a Norse settlement dating from the 9th century. Waterford has long been associated with fine glassware. In the early part of the 19th century heavy duties brought about the virtual closure of the industry but it has now been revived and enjoys an enviable reputation throughout the world.

Powerscourt House Gardens, Co. Wicklow *overleaf.* The huge demesne of Powerscourt stands to the south of Enniskerry, in charming and picturesque countryside. Originally the home of the Powerscourt family, the outstanding gardens are now open to the public and attract many thousands of visitors each year.

Offering outstanding natural beauty in one of the loveliest of the glens of Wicklow, the Glendalough waterfall *left* may be seen on one of the many woodland walks in the area, as may the remains of an early Irish Monastery.

Across the lake, *right* may be seen the original house, the home of the Powerscourt family, from which the estate takes its name; the Demesne of Powerscourt.

Besides being set in an area of great natural beauty, the extensive gardens of Powerscourt have been superbly landscaped—as is evident from the previous page—but there are still many charming corners to be found *below* both in the grounds of the estate and in the surrounding countryside.

The peace and tranquillity of the lovely Vale of Clara *overleaf* is quite unforgettable. Situated close to the village of Rathdrum, Co. Wicklow, and the Wicklow Mountains, the whole area is renowned as a touring centre, and justifiably so.

Clew Bay *top left* from Westport, Co. Mayo. Once famous as a port, the coming of the railway brought about the transformation of Westport into the fishing centre it has now become. It is very well situated on the banks of a stream which flows into the island-studded bay.

Typical of so many, all over Ireland, a croft *bottom left* on the Cliften Road by the River Erriff, Westport, Co. Mayo.

Westport House, Co. Mayo *above* is a Georgian mansion dating from 1730, which was designed by Richard Cassels and James Wyatt. It stands in its own estate, just by the Carrowbeg River, and belongs to the Marquis of Sligo.

Achill Island, Co. Mayo is the largest island off the Irish coast and may be reached from the mainland by means of a swivel bridge. The hilly island affords, particularly on the north and west coasts, some magnificent scenery. In the south-east corner of the island stands the keep of Kildownet Castle. The village of Menawn is now a centre for shark fishing, which has grown into a considerable industry.

Dungory Castle *below* has, fairly recently, been completely restored and is now in use once again as a residence. The castle was originally built in the 16th century and stands on an islet of Kinvarra Bay, close to the small port of Kinvarra.

Freehold village *right* is on the coast of Co. Clare, ne Lidoonvarna. On clear days, as is shown in the picture, t distant coast of Connemara may be clearly seen.

With the Atlantic ocean beneath them, the magnificent Clif of Moher, Co. Clare extend for some five miles along t coast, and are considered to be one of Ireland's major scen attractions, particularly to the ornithologist and t geologist.

Facing onto the River Liffey are two of Dublin's finest and most impressive buildings, the Custom House *top right,* and the Four Courts *bottom right.* The Custom House is the work of James Gandon. It was completed in 1791 and is considered to be the finest example of his work. The Four Courts was completed five years later, in 1796 and, again, was the work of James Gandon–this time in cooperation with Thomas Cooley.

The Capital of the Republic of Ireland, Dublin is a very beautiful city set in lovely countryside in Dublin Bay. The River Liffey flows through the heart of the city, crossed by many fine bridges. The finest of these is, without doubt O'Connell Bridge *overleaf.* The bridge stands at the foot of O'Connell Street *above* with its solid and impressive statue of the great man. The statue, by Foley, was erected in 1882.

Player's Please
BEA
Europe's foremost airline
Fly
ULSTER BANK
CONFECTIONS

Often described as one of the outstanding beauty spots in all Ireland, Glengarriff—the name means 'Rugged Glen'—is in Co. Cork. Quite close to Glengarriff is Garinish Island with its beautiful, formal Italian Gardens *left* and martello tower. It was in these gardens that George Bernard Shaw wrote part of his play 'Saint Joan'.

Cobh, Co. Cork, is the main Irish port of call for transatlantic liners. Standing on a hill above the harbour is the Roman Catholic Cathedral of St. Colman *right,* a building in the Gothic style, which was completed in 1919.

Bantry town and the bay *bottom left and overleaf* seen from Sherkin View, Co. Cork. Bantry has a harbour which accommodates a number of coastal vessels but its main industries are now connected with woollen and linen manufacturing. Lord Bantry's beautiful Georgian mansion nearby is famous for its art treasures which may be viewed by the public at specified times.

Gougane Barra, Co. Cork *below* is a beautiful lake surrounded on three sides by towering mountains. The lake is fed by the numerous small streams flowing down the mountainsides and the lake, in its turn, feeds, and is, indeed, the source of, the River Lee.

In a picturesque setting above the Eske stands Donegal Castle *left*. It was originally the castle of the O'Donnells and dates from 1474. Parts of the original were incorporated into the later castle which was built in 1610 by Sir Basil Brooke. Much of the castle is now in ruins but enough of it remains to provide a fascinating link with Ireland's past.

Still using the time-honoured and hard-working donkey, an elderly Irish peasant *right* pictured in Co. Galway.

One of the most beautiful inlets on the Irish coast is to be found at Killary Harbour *below*. It extends inland for some eight miles and is very popular with visitors, for whom it provides excellent sailing and boating facilities.

The ancient ruins of Monasterboice monastery stand in a churchyard *above* on the main Dundalk to Drogheda road. It is noted, in particular, for its High Crosses, the most interesting of which is the cross of Muiredach, pictured here, which dates from the 10th century.

Clonmacnoise is situated almost in the exact centre of Ireland, in Co. Offaly. There are many notable buildings and ruins to be seen here in addition to some very early grave slabs. Notable among the ruins is O Rourke's Tower, *right*, seen here from the cathedral doorway.

Killarney is noted throughout the world as Ireland's main beauty spot and tourist centre. The lakes *top right* in particular were described by Sir Walter Scott as "The grandest sight I have ever seen". An excursion down the lakes is an experience not to be missed by any visitor to the area. Horse-drawn vehicles, of which there are many, are very popular with tourists and are an ideal and liesurely way to visit the many notable places. One of these is Kate Kearney's Cottage *below* which stands in rocky Gap of Dunloe.

Some idea of the beauty of Ireland's coastline may be seen from the picture *overleaf* of Derrynane Bay, taken from Coomakista Pass, Co. Kerry. Nearby lies the charming village of Caherdaniel.

Ireland has no coal of its own and peat is heavily relied on as fuel and is particularly common in many of Ireland's cottage homes. Peat is, in fact, coal in its first stages of development. It is found in marshy areas which are so typical of parts of Ireland. Peat cutting is still carried out in much the same, traditional, way as these pictures in Co. Kerry *above* and Co. Galway *right* clearly show.

The coastal road which carries the traveller around the shores of the lovely Iveragh peninsula in Co. Kerry is known as the Ring of Kerry. The views from the road are magnificent *overleaf* and include such scenes as Macgillicuddy's Reeks—Ireland's highest mountain.

The mountains around the Lakes of Killarney in Co. Kerry are separated by the Gap of Dunloe *left* which cuts between the Tomies and the Purple Mountain, and the main range of Macgillicuddy's Reeks.

A typical whitewashed cottage and its farm-yard *right* near Dingle in Co. Kerry. Dingle's name means 'The Fortress' and it was, indeed, the site of a fort even before the arrival of the Anglo-Normans. Another claim to fame that Dingle enjoys is that of being the most westerly town in Europe.

Cattle casually wander along the fine beach *below* at West Cove which, together with Castle Cove, both in Co. Kerry, are splendid little seaside resorts on a bay of the Kenmare River, easily reached by the coastal road, or Ring of Kerry.

In the 13th century the Cistercians founded Hore Abbey *above* at Cashel, on the Tipperary plain. The name Cashel means 'Stone Fort' and it was on the famous rock at Cashel that the King of Munster erected, in the 5th century, the fort from which the town takes its name. It was in this fort that St. Patrick preached when he was in the area.

The oldest building in Cashel is the 85 feet high Round Tower *left* which is believed to date from the 10th century. The Tower shares the Rock of Cashel with the Cathedral, Cormac's Chapel and the Cross of Cashel.

In the Glen of Aherlow, in Co. Tipperary, there stands, on the lower slopes of the mountain known as Slievenamuck, a 16 feet high statue of Christ the King. The commanding view from the site of the statue across this remote glen is well illustrated *right*. In days gone by the Fitzpatricks and the O Briens staged many a bloody battle for possession of this important pass between the Vale of Tipperary and Cork.

Another of Ireland's many beauty spots is to be found in the area of Drumcliff, Co. Sligo. To the east of Drumcliff lies the beautiful Glencar Lough *above* with King's Mount rising majestically in the background.

Sometimes described as Ireland's 'Table Mountain' is Benbulben Mountain *top right*. Benbulben is noted both for the fine viewpoint it affords and for the profusion of alpine flora which are to be found there. It also epitomises, in this particular picture, Ireland's other title of 'The Emerald Isle'. The mountain is seen again *bottom right* with Sligo town in the foreground.

Situated on the famed Galway Bay, the city of Galway is full of interest and provides an excellent starting point for touring the splendid surrounding countryside. One of its notable landmarks, though by no means as old as many of the others, is the Salmon Weir Bridge *above* of 1818.

Ireland is noted the world over for its pastures, which play their part, not only in the breeding of fine horses, but also in the production of some of the world's best dairy produce *top right*.

The River Barrow with, in the background, Brandon Hil Near this lovely view the river passes through the town of New Ross, in Co. Wexford. New Ross is particularl interesting for the 'Three Bullet Gate'. During th Cromwellian Wars the town suffered badly and, during fierce bombardment, three cannon balls lodged in one of th gates and it is from this event that the gate now takes it name.

Many of the visitors who come to Ireland each year do so for the peace and quiet for which the island is noted. It is fitting, therefore, that the last picture in this book should feature just such a simple pleasure; a jaunting car making its way along the lovely shore of the Killarney Lakes.